Lerner SPORTS

SPORTS
ALL-STARS

PATRICK
MAHOMES

Jon M. Fishman

Lerner Publications ◆ Minneapolis

Lerner Publications Company
An imprint of Lerner Publishing Group, Inc.
241 First Avenue North
Minneapolis, MN 55401 USA

For reading levels and more information, look up this title at www.lernerbooks.com.

Main body text set in Albany Std.
Typeface provided by Agfa.

Library of Congress Cataloging-in-Publication Data

Names: Fishman, Jon M., author.
Title: Patrick Mahomes / Jon M. Fishman.
Description: Minneapolis : Lerner Publications, 2020. | Series: Sports all-stars | Includes bibliographical references and index. | Audience: Age 7–11. | Audience: Grade 4 to 6.
Identifiers: LCCN 2018060926 (print) | LCCN 2018061510 (ebook) | ISBN 9781541578487 (eb pdf) | ISBN 9781541578463 (lb : alk. paper) | ISBN 9781541578470 (pb : alk. paper)
Subjects: LCSH: Mahomes, Patrick, 1995– —Juvenile literature. | Quarterbacks (Football)—United States—Biography—Juvenile literature. | Kansas City Chiefs (Football team)—Juvenile literature.
Classification: LCC GV939.M284 (ebook) | LCC GV939.M284 F57 2020 (print) | DDC 796.332092 [B]—dc23

LC record available at https://lccn.loc.gov/2018060926

Manufactured in the United States of America
1-46972-47831-4/12/2019

CONTENTS

THROWING STAR

Patrick Mahomes drops back to pass during a game against the Pittsburgh Steelers.

Kansas City Chiefs quarterback Patrick Mahomes wasn't supposed to be so good so soon. Quarterbacks often take a long time to adjust to the new challenges that come with playing in the National Football League (NFL).

FACTS
AT A GLANCE

- **Date of Birth:** September 17, 1995

- **Position:** quarterback

- **League:** NFL

- **Professional Highlights:** chosen by the Kansas City Chiefs with the 10th overall pick in the 2017 **draft**, set an all-time record with 10 touchdowns in the first two games of a season, won the NFL Most Valuable Player (MVP) Award and the Offensive Player of the Year Award in 2018

- **Personal Highlights:** learned about pro sports from his father, a pro baseball pitcher, gives part of the credit for his arm strength to throwing baseballs with his father, loves to connect with people and charities in Kansas City

They aren't supposed to set all-time passing records in their third start. But that's what happened when the Chiefs met the Pittsburgh Steelers on September 16, 2018.

Mahomes and the Chiefs were on fire in the first quarter. Mahomes threw three touchdown passes to three different wide receivers. But everything changed in the second quarter. Steelers quarterback Ben Roethlisberger matched Mahomes with three touchdown passes of his own. The score was tied at halftime 21–21.

The second half started with a long 25-yard touchdown throw by Mahomes. Then the Steelers scored to tie the game again. Less than two minutes later, Mahomes hurled yet another scoring pass.

Mahomes throws a pass against the Pittsburgh Steelers.

The Pittsburgh Steelers formed in 1933. Since then, only two players have ever thrown six touchdowns against them in a game: Jim Kelly in 1991 and Mahomes in 2018.

It was his fifth touchdown of the game, and it gave Kansas City a seven-point lead. Mahomes threw another touchdown in the fourth quarter. Pittsburgh kept scoring, but the Chiefs held on to win 42–37.

Mahomes tossed six touchdowns in the game. He had four touchdown passes the previous week in a win against the Los Angeles Chargers. That gave him a record-setting 10 touchdowns in the first two games of the season. No quarterback in NFL history had ever thrown that many combined touchdowns that early in the season before. Mahomes was setting records despite playing just a few games in the league. Fans and teammates couldn't wait to see what he'd do next.

CHOOSING WISELY

Pat Mahomes, Patrick's father, pitched for six different MLB teams in 11 seasons.

Patrick Mahomes was born on September 17, 1995, in Tyler, Texas. He spent a lot of time on pro baseball fields as a child.

New York Mets pitcher Mike Hampton (rear) and Patrick both try to catch a ball during a Mets practice in 2000.

That's because his father, Pat, was a Major League Baseball (MLB) player.

Baseball became Patrick's favorite sport. His dad helped feed his passion. "I bought him a plastic bat with one of those little balls and he would never go to bed," his father said. "He would always want to hit with it." Patrick sometimes joined his dad on the field to warm up before MLB games. The boy began catching **fly balls** hit by pro baseball players when he was just six years old.

Patrick loved to compete, and he always tried to win. He shined as a pitcher on his high school's baseball team. Patrick also starred on the school's basketball team and liked soccer, golf, **table tennis**, and football. Pat thought his son's future was in baseball or basketball. He worried that Patrick would get hurt if he kept playing football.

But Patrick didn't want to give up football. His goal was to play quarterback. At first, his football coaches thought he would be better at other positions. But Patrick kept trying. He became the high school team's quarterback as a junior in 2012. He threw 46 touchdown passes and just nine **interceptions** that year. He also passed for 3,839 yards. It was clear that Patrick had a future in football.

Patrick was a star quarterback for his high school team.

Patrick looks for a receiver while playing for Texas Tech.

His senior season was even better. He threw 50 touchdowns and six interceptions, and passed for 4,619 yards. He loved playing quarterback, but he had a big decision to make. MLB's Detroit Tigers chose Patrick in the 37th round of the 2014 draft. It was time to decide if he'd follow his father into baseball or choose his own path and play football.

Mahomes chose football. He enrolled at Texas Tech University in Lubbock, Texas. He spent three years at Texas Tech and got better every season. His touchdown throws and yards passing rose each year. The NFL took notice.

On April 27, 2017, Mahomes gathered with a large group of friends and family in Tyler. The group clapped and cheered as the Kansas City Chiefs selected Mahomes. He was the 10th overall pick in the NFL Draft. The team had traded two future draft picks to move up in the draft order. It was a huge price to pay to get Mahomes. The Chiefs were sure he would be a superstar.

Mahomes puts on a Kansas City Chiefs hat after being selected in the NFL Draft.

Mahomes tosses the ball during warm-ups.

One reason the Chiefs were so confident in Mahomes was his powerful arm. He can throw a football more than 75 yards down the field.

Mahomes drops back to pass during practice.

He began building his arm strength as a kid by playing catch with his dad and practicing like the pros.

Many pro baseball players use a **drill** called long toss. Two people stand at a distance and throw a baseball back and forth. After a few minutes, they move farther apart and keep throwing. The throwers move farther away from each other a few times before moving closer again. Mahomes says he began playing long toss when he was five years old with his father. "So me doing that all the time, it just built arm strength," he said.

Years of playing competitive sports made Mahomes strong. He became even stronger during special training sessions in 2017. Before the NFL Draft, he worked out at a training center in San Diego, California. He lifted weights and learned about the importance of healthful food.

Mahomes thought weighing less would help him run faster during games. To lose a few pounds, he ran on a **treadmill** while wearing a heavy vest. He also studied football plays during his time in San Diego. Coaches told him what to expect as an NFL **rookie**.

Mahomes warms up with teammates during training camp.

Workouts were just as intense once Mahomes joined the Chiefs. The team played its first game of the 2018 regular season on September 9. But Mahomes had arrived at **training camp** over a month earlier. It was time to work. "The grind of training camp is real," Mahomes said. "You have to come in every single day and get better."

Mahomes throws a lot during training camp so he's ready for the season.

In 2017, Mahomes threw a football 62 miles (100 km) per hour during a special TV event. That's as fast as some of the hardest-throwing quarterbacks in NFL history threw a football.

Most training camp days begin with an early breakfast followed by weight lifting. Then players may meet with their coaches. They talk about game plans or watch video of previous games and practices.

Next is the first practice of the day. Mahomes and his teammates practice plays and run drills. A second practice later is often more physical. The players wear all their gear and crash into one another at nearly full speed. Through it all, Mahomes throws pass after pass. He throws hundreds of footballs to teammates and coaches each day. When training camp ends, he's ready to take on the world's toughest players in the NFL.

Mahomes serves a meal to Kansas City fans.

Mahomes throws out the first pitch at a Kansas City Royals baseball game in 2018.

Mahomes enjoys life in Kansas City on and off the field. After his rookie year ended in January 2018, he stayed in the city for much of the **off-season**. He wanted to explore his new home.

Kansas City is famous for **barbecued** food. Mahomes ate at different barbecue restaurants but said he couldn't choose a favorite. He went to an auto race at Kansas

Speedway and attended baseball and soccer games. Supporting other teams and spending time with people in Kansas City is important to Mahomes. The community strongly supports the Chiefs, and he wants to return the favor. "That's big for me to give back and try to build a relationship with the community and especially the kids," he said.

Mahomes surprises a group of KC United! youth football players with a holiday shopping spree.

Helping Wounded Warriors

Mahomes works to help veterans in his community. Veterans of war may suffer from post-traumatic stress disorder. This serious condition can cause anxiety and nightmares. It can prevent some veterans from working, making it hard to pay for a place to live. That's when Mahomes and Veterans Community Project step in. The group seeks to help all homeless veterans find places to live.

In October 2018, Mahomes and other volunteers helped build small homes for veterans in Kansas City. The homes

This veteran's home was built as part of the Veterans Community Project.

are safe places for veterans to live and adjust to life after the military. Mahomes doesn't have much experience building homes, so he spent most of his time painting.

Mahomes runs with the ball during a game against the Baltimore Ravens.

Mahomes connects with kids by working with youth football players. He teaches them about life in the NFL and gives them tips to improve. That's just one way Mahomes gives back.

On December 9, 2018, the Chiefs played the Baltimore Ravens in Kansas City. Mahomes and other Chiefs players wore shoes with special designs. The designs brought attention to causes that were important to the players. For Mahomes, that was Team Luke—Hope for Minds. The group supports children with brain injuries. Artist John Sebelius designed the red, green, and sparkling-white shoes that Mahomes wore. "Patrick Mahomes was totally okay with glitter so that's why his are a little bit more bedazzled," Sebelius said.

Mahomes wore shoes to support Team Luke in a game against the Baltimore Ravens.

SUPER BOWL GOALS

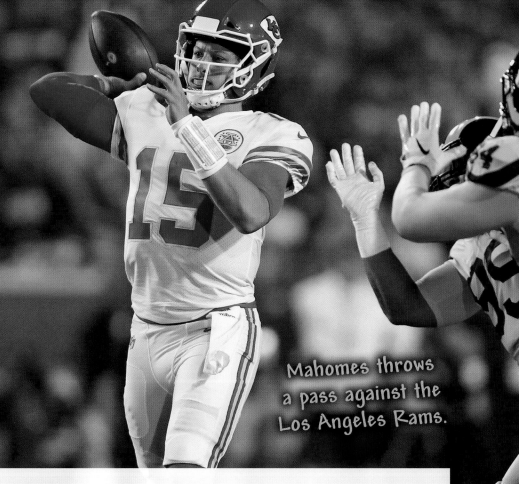

Mahomes throws a pass against the Los Angeles Rams.

Mahomes was a backup quarterback in 2017, and he played in just one game as a rookie. By the second game of the 2018 season, he was setting records and entertaining Chiefs fans with amazing throws.

Mahomes's success has made him popular with Kansas City fans.

His six-touchdown game against the Steelers was just the beginning of an incredible year.

In November, Mahomes threw six scoring passes again in a game against the Los Angeles Rams. Steelers quarterback Ben Roethlisberger is the only other player to have two six-touchdown games in the same season. Mahomes led Kansas City to one of the best records in the NFL in 2018.

Mahomes poses with the 2018 NFL Player of the Year Award.

As the Chiefs rose in the standings, the quarterback's popularity rose with fans. Sales of Mahomes jerseys and other products soared. After the season, Mahomes won the NFL Most Valuable Player and Offensive Player of the Year awards.

Fans love to watch quarterbacks throw touchdown passes. And Mahomes has shown that he can throw with the best of them. But he also knows that his success is tied to his team's success. That's why winning the NFL's top prize is his goal. "The next step is the Super Bowl," he said.

Mahomes celebrates after throwing a touchdown pass in the 2019 NFL Pro Bowl.

All-Star Stats

In his short time in the **NFL**, **Patrick Mahomes** has proven to be great at a very important skill. He throws more touchdown passes than anyone else does. Look at how he ranked in scoring throws during the 2018–2019 season:

Player	Team	Touchdown Passes
Patrick Mahomes	Kansas City Chiefs	50
Andrew Luck	Indianapolis Colts	39
Matt Ryan	Atlanta Falcons	35
Russell Wilson	Seattle Seahawks	35
Ben Roethlisberger	Pittsburgh Steelers	34
Jared Goff	Los Angeles Rams	32
Philip Rivers	Los Angeles Chargers	32
Drew Brees	New Orleans Saints	32
Kirk Cousins	Minnesota Vikings	30
Tom Brady	New England Patriots	29

Source Notes

9   Nicholas Talbot, "In the Spotlight: Mahomes' Childhood Prepared Him for Big Stage at Tech," *Lubbock Avalanche-Journal*, September 11, 2015, https://www.lubbockonline.com/sports-red-raiders -football/2015-09-11/spotlight-mahomes-childhood -prepared-him-big-stage-tech.

14 Brandon Hall, "The Childhood Drill That Helped Patrick Mahomes Build Superhuman Arm Strength," *Stack*, last modified January 10, 2019, https://www .stack.com/a/the-childhood-drill-that-helped-pat -mahomes-build-superhuman-arm-strength.

16 Robert Rimpson, "Chiefs QB Patrick Mahomes Ready for the Grind of Training Camp," Chiefs Wire, July 23, 2018, https://chiefswire.usatoday .com/2018/07/23/chiefs-qb-patrick-mahomes-ready -for-the-grind-of-training-camp/.

20 Matt Conner, "Patrick Mahomes Interview: Chiefs Quarterback on Superstition and K.C. Barbecue," Arrowhead Addict, accessed December 9, 2018, https://arrowheadaddict.com/2018/02/09/patrick -mahomes-interview-kansas-city-chiefs-alex-smith -eric-bieniemy/.

23 "Chiefs Unveil Cleats Players Will Wear Sunday for Special 'My Cause, My Cleats' Game," *Fox 4 Kansas City*, December 6, 2018, https://fox4kc. com/2018/12/06/chiefs-unveil-cleats-players-will -wear-sunday-for-special-my-cause-my-cleats-game/.

27 Pete Sweeney, "Patrick Mahomes: 'The Next Step Is the Super Bowl,'" Arrowhead Pride, May 4, 2018, https://www.arrowheadpride.com/2018/5/4/17319558 /patrick-mahomes-the-next-step-is-the-super-bowl.

barbecued: cooked over a source of heat such as hot coals

draft: an event in which teams take turns choosing new players

drill: an exercise designed to improve a skill

fly balls: baseballs that are batted high into the air and soar to the outfield

interceptions: passes caught by the other team that result in a change of possession

off-season: the time of year when a sports league doesn't play games

rookie: a first-year player

table tennis: a game similar to tennis that is played on a table with paddles

training camp: the time before the season when NFL teams get ready to play games

treadmill: a machine with a spinning belt used to run in place

Further Information

Chiefs Home
https://www.chiefs.com

Football: National Football League
http://www.ducksters.com/sports/national_football_league.php

Monson, James. *Behind the Scenes Football*. Minneapolis:
Lerner Publications, 2020.

Morey, Allan. *The Kansas City Chiefs Story*. Minneapolis:
Bellwether Media, 2017.

Patrick Mahomes Volunteers to Help Veterans
https://awesome98.com/patrick-mahomes-volunteers-to-help
-veterans-video/

Savage, Jeff. *Football Super Stats*. Minneapolis: Lerner
Publications, 2018.

Index

Photo Acknowledgments

Image credits: Justin K. Aller/Getty Images, p. 4; AP Photo/Gene J. Puskar, p. 6; Matthew Stockman/Allsport/Getty Images, p. 8; AP Photo/Kathy Willens, p. 9; AP Photo/Tyler Morning Helegraph, Victor Texcucano, p. 10; Jerod Foster/Icon Sportswire/Getty Images, p. 11; AP Photo/Chelsea Purgahn/Tyler Morning Telegraph, p. 12; David Eulitt/Getty Images, p. 13; Scott Winters/Icon Sportswire/Getty Images, p. 14; AP Photo/Charlie Riedel, pp. 15, 22; AP Photo/Charlie Neibergall, p. 16; Colin Braley/AP Images for Dixie Ultra®, p. 18; John Sleezer/Kansas City Star/TNS /Alamy Live News, p. 19; Colin Braley/AP Images for DICK'S Sporting Goods, p. 20; Christopher Smith/For The Washington Post/Getty Images, p. 21; Peter Aiken/ Stringer/Getty Images, p. 23; Sean M. Haffey/Getty Images, p. 24; AP Photo/Reed Hoffmann, p. 25; Omar Vega/AP Images for FedEx, p. 26; Jamie Squire/Getty Images, p. 27.

Cover Image: Peter G. Aiken/Getty Images.